Instant Insight

Instant Insight

200 Ways to Create
the Life You Really Want

Jonathan Robinson

Health Communications, Inc.
Deerfield Beach, Florida

Library of Congress Cataloging-in-Publication Data

Robinson, Jonathan, (date)
   Instant Insight: 200 ways to create the life you really want/Jonathan Robinson.
     p. cm.
   ISBN 9041109161
   1. Self-actualization (Psychology) 2. Self-management (Psychology) 3. Conduct of life. I. Title.
   BF637.S4R59 1996
   158'.1--DC20

                                          96-22278
                                            CIP

Publisher: Health Communications, Inc.
                3201 S.W. 15th Street
                Deerfield Beach, Florida 33442-8190

Cover design by Lawna Patterson Oldfield
Cover illustration ©1996 Master Series Illustration Library

*This book is
dedicated to the part of
YOU that desires to create a
life filled with love, harmony
and alignment with your
higher purpose.*

Contents

Acknowledgments

S ince this book is about personal growth and creating a fulfilling life, I first want to thank those people who have been most instrumental in my own growth. Early on, Brian Strehlke helped entice me out of my shell. Later, Justin Gold, Joyce Walton and Ram Dass helped propel me into "other worlds." Tony Robbins introduced me to the power of questions. I thank you all for your contributions to my life. And the love of my sweetheart, Helena, and the indwelling Spirit motivate me to keep growing toward greater joy and wonder.

For the I.C.A.N. method outlined in this book, I want to thank Simon D'Arcy, Bruce Randall and David Sampanis for their contributions. My family and friends have all been very supportive of my goals. I am ever grateful to all of you.

> *The next message you need is always right where you are.*
>
> —Ram Dass

According to an ancient Eastern story, one day the gods were discussing where they should hide Truth so human beings would not find it so easily. If people found truth too easily, the gods were afraid they would have little to keep themselves amused. One god put forth, "Let's hide Truth on top of the highest mountain. That way, only the most disciplined and strong will be able to find Truth." Another god countered, "Let's hide Truth in the deepest, darkest cave. That way, only the bravest will find Truth." But the wisest of the gods laughed and said, "It is not necessary to hide Truth on top of a mountain or in a cave. All we need do is hide Truth within each person's own heart. That is the last place human beings would think to look."

I believe we all have a storehouse of wisdom within us. Unfortunately, we get distracted from listening to and acting upon the truths that are within our own hearts. We turn to books, therapists and friends for answers that can only come from our own selves. So how can we quickly and easily access this inner wisdom? By asking the right questions. Asking ourselves a good question is like having a truly helpful psychotherapy session, but without all the expense.

I know the power of questions because I've used certain questions to dramatically change the course of my life. As a teenager, I was painfully shy. In fact, I rarely spoke to anyone. I didn't have a single friend. Inside my head I would continually think, "What if I say something and I sound like a fool?" By focusing on this negative question, I became paralyzed with fear in social situations. One day, grace descended on me in the form of a question. While seeing a new kid in class, I thought to myself, "What interesting things might I learn about this person?" When I focused in this new positive way, I became less self-conscious. When I ventured to ask this classmate about himself, we made a real nice connection. I had my first friend. Soon, I was asking others all sorts of thought-provoking questions, and I made many more friends. Eventually, my curiosity about other people led to my occupation as a psychotherapist and author. Asking myself a different question changed my life.

Typically, psychotherapists are portrayed as spending their days listening to people's problems. But that's not why we get paid $50 to $150 an hour. After all, a friend can listen to your problems for free. The reason psychotherapists get paid so much is that they ask their clients specific questions to help them access their own unique wisdom. The problem is, without the right questions, we can become focused on beliefs and behaviors that fail to get us what we really want. On the other hand, *with* the right questions, we have the power to hear our inner wisdom and create our lives the way we desire.

Over the last 20 years, I have been a self-help book junkie. I've read hundreds of books about everything from how to have great relationships to easy ways to make millions of dollars. Fortunately, almost all the self-help books I've read have come to the same conclusion. They all basically say success comes from focusing your mind in ways that lead to better decisions and more effective behavior. How can that be done? I have found that asking good questions is the easiest and quickest way to make better evaluations, and thereby better decisions. As we change our mental focus, we see things that were invisible to us before. We learn to focus on what we *ultimately* want, such as feelings of love, peace and joy. Soon enough, what we focus on grows.

The lyrics to the Bruce Springsteen song "Hungry Heart" talk about flowing like a river, procceding down the wrong path full steam ahead. When it comes to checking on how our life, relationships, health and other matters are going, we rarely look to see where we're headed. Perhaps we think about such things once or twice a year, but that's not enough. If you checked to see if your car was headed in the right direction only once a year, you'd certainly crash. Questions help us stay on course in life, or gently move us back on track when we've fallen off our desired path.

How to Use This Book

Think of this book as an encyclopedia for how to successfully deal with any situation in your life. If you're interested in learning how to get better control of your finances, read the chapters dealing with career and money. If you're feeling dissatisfied with your love life, go to the chapter on relationships. When you find the appropriate section, you'll find a list of thought-provoking questions. Unlike most self-help books, you'll find no advice or answers. The best answers are conveniently placed in an easy-to-reach location—inside you. All that's needed are the right questions to help trigger your intuitive, innate wisdom. When you find a question that calls to you and your current life situation, take some time with it. Meditate on it. Let the question sink into the depths of your being. When the appropriate answer arrives, it will feel like you have found something that was temporarily lost.

There are several ways you can use the questions in this book for your benefit. Many people find that writing down their answers in a journal helps them to explore their thoughts more thoroughly. In addition, writing down your answers allows you to refer back to your initial insights for later use. Another way to use this book is to have a friend or family member ask the questions you're interested in pursuing. Sharing your answers with someone you trust can lead to additional insights, feedback and intimacy.

When contemplating these questions, allow yourself to use both your rational *and* intuitive abilities to come up with the best possible answer(s). To tap into your intuition, it's helpful to first take time to quiet your mind. I believe each person knows of an activity that helps him or her to feel peaceful inside. For some, it may be spending time in nature or going for a walk. For others, it could be spending quiet time in meditation or prayer, or listening to music. Once your mind is quiet, it will be easier to know when an answer to a question truly feels *right*. While the rational mind figures things out through a linear thought process, our intuitive mind knows things by how they *feel*. After asking a question and listening inside for an answer, notice what your "gut" feeling is. With a little practice, you'll soon be able to decipher the "voice" of true intuitive guidance.

Answers can come in different ways. Sometimes the "right" answer will appear instantly—as if from nowhere. Other answers may take a few days to congeal before they "instantaneously" pop into your head. I've even had the answer to a question come to me from a roadside billboard passed in traffic, and it's not uncommon for a friend to blurt out advice that is a perfect answer to a question I've been contemplating. I've also heard people say answers have come to them in their dreams, or through an inner prompting to take one course of action over another.

You'll notice that many of the questions in this book can be answered in more than one manner. It can be fun to come up with at least five answers to a single question and then choose the answer(s) you like the best. I have found the first thing that comes to my mind is not always the best. By aiming for a high *quantity* of answers, creative thinking can be stimulated. I've seen that the fourth or fifth answer I think of has often proved to be the best solution to my problem.

You may also choose to use this book as a useful aid with the people you love. If someone comes to you with a problem, look up the appropriate section and see if you can ask them a useful question. You've probably noticed that trying to give people advice rarely, if ever, works. People feel belittled when they have to listen to advice. But people like answering questions. When you ask someone a question, you're indirectly saying you trust that person's ability to come up with the right answer. I've been amazed at how easily people can solve problems simply by answering a thought-provoking question.

Once you've found the questions that are especially suitable to you, *circle them* so they can be easily located whenever you need them. I think you'll find it more valuable if you focus on answering just a few questions really well, rather than trying to answer a lot of questions in a superficial manner. Spend quality time with the questions you find most helpful. A question that calls to your current life situation is like a trusted friend guiding you to the wisdom deep within you. Rather than read this book in a linear manner, feel free to skip around to the chapters and questions that are of greatest interest to you.

The answers you receive to some of these questions may require you to change long-held behaviors in your life. Changing harmful habits and behaviors is always difficult at first. To help you act in alignment with the answers you receive to these questions, I suggest you carefully read chapter 14. Here I reveal a technique that will greatly help you act on whatever wisdom you receive. This method is so powerful that in my experience, it is 10 times more effective than any other motivation technique. If you use it, I'm confident you'll be able to consistently take action for creating the life you *really* want.

I wish you the best in exploring all the wisdom within you, and I hope the answers and actions that result bring you much love, serenity and joy in your life.

2

Intimate
Relationships

*When two people are at one in their
inmost hearts, they shatter even
the strength of iron . . .*

—Excerpt from the *I Ching*

The results are in. Intimate relationships in this country are in a state of free fall. Nowadays, a full 50 percent of people getting married will eventually divorce. Even many of the couples that remain married have severe difficulty. It need not be this way. In my counseling practice, I am privy to seeing the mistakes couples repeatedly make. Fortunately, I have found that when clients are informed of how to ask the right questions, they can easily avoid most of the problems they've encountered in previous relationships. In addition, in my own relationship I have found that there are certain questions that help keep love vibrantly alive, even after many years of partnership.

If questions are so effective in avoiding difficulty or keeping love alive, why don't we use them more often? We don't use them because we get caught up in other things. For example, when we become infatuated upon first meeting someone, our rationality is put on hold. Love not only makes us blind, it can make us stupid as well. We don't think to ask questions that would help us evaluate if a partner is appropriate for us. When our hearts are swept away, we fail to consider what problems we may face with this person later on. That is why it's a good idea to have a list of questions prepared beforehand. When you find yourself swept off your feet, the right questions can help you keep at least one foot on the ground.

In trying to keep love alive in a long-term partnership, the biggest enemy is that of taking each other for granted. That's why we need something to propel ourselves out of mental ruts and find ever-new ways of appreciating and loving our partner. Questions can help keep our minds focused on love and romance, despite the ravaging effects of time, stress and day-to-day distraction. Whether looking for a partner, considering what to do with a partner, or trying to re-ignite a long-term relationship, I think you'll find many helpful ideas to consider in the following questions.

Finding an Appropriate Partner:

Most people don't choose a partner, they "fall" for one. When people fall, they can get hurt. The questions that follow are designed to help you choose more wisely and avoid some of the difficulties you may have had in the past. In addition, there are questions to help direct you toward appropriate places to find the person you've been hoping for.

1) *What are the five most important characteristics I want to have in a potential mate?*

2) *What are three characteristics in a potential mate I want to make sure I avoid?*

3) *What type of person have I been attracted to in the past that was not good for me?*

4) *Where would people appropriate for me be likely to spend their free time?*

A female friend of mine once gave me a valuable tip about finding an intimate partner. She said the secret is to go to places where there are a lot of people of the opposite sex, and few people of the same sex as you. In her case, she met her boyfriend in an auto shop class. There were 28 guys and her. The guys were practically lining up to date her, which made her look pretty good. After a couple of dates with different guys, she settled on the man she wanted.

5) *Where could I go or what classes could I take where there would be a lot of people of the opposite sex?*

6) *Whom do I know who might have a friend or acquaintance who would be a good match for me? Have I told them I'm interested in meeting new men or women?*

7) *What clubs, groups, classes or organizations could I join that might have interesting people to meet?*

Interviewing a Possible Partner:

When you meet a potential partner, it's a good idea to see if it's more than just a match based on chemical infatuation. The best way to do that is to "interview" them. As part of your second, third or fourth date, casually ask them questions that will help you evaluate if they are an appropriate partner for you. Find out what their interests are, what their relationship history is, how sane they are. When taking a job, we ask questions about the company. When considering a lifetime partner, it makes sense to know who we're really dealing with before giving our heart away. By asking the following questions amid normal conversation, you'll learn many important things about your date. In some cases, the answers you receive could keep you from falling for the wrong person.

1) *What do you like to do in your free time?*

2) *What's most important in your life right now?*

3) *Have you had many relationships in the past? Have you ever been married?*

4) *Do you ever want to have kids?*

5) *How long have you been out of a steady relationship?*

I was on a date with a beautiful woman, and I was quite infatuated. I couldn't tell if I was in love with her looks, her soul, or both. I began to ask questions about her past. In talking about her previous boyfriend, she said, "He was such a jerk. I could never trust him. I haven't even said hello to him since the day I left him." I casually inquired about the boyfriend before him. Her reply was, "Oh, that loser—he was really a joke. I'm glad I ditched him." Spontaneously, her remarks gave me a vision. I could see myself having a tumultuous relationship with her and then being unceremoniously dumped after a few months. Then I pictured her on a date with some future guy who asks her, "How about the last guy you dated?" Her reply would be, "What a Bozo he was . . ." To avoid the pain of being part of her established history of "losers," I decided not to go out with her again.

6) *Why did your last relationship end? Are you still friendly with the person?*

7) *Have you ever gone to relationship counseling, or something like that?*

8) *What's your family like? Are you close to your mother and father?*

Questions to Ask Your Partner to
Help Keep Your Love Alive:

To avoid the mental ruts that inevitably creep into long-term relationships, the following questions are invaluable. They serve as reminders that loving communication is continuously necessary in order to keep the heart open.

1) *What helps you to feel most loved by me?*

2) *Do you know what it is you do that makes me feel most loved?*

In an attempt to become a better partner, one day I decided to contact two previous girlfriends and ask them what they liked and didn't like about being in a relationship with me. When it got to the subject of sex, one of them said, "I never liked how you would lick my ear when we were sexually intimate. That's one of the main reasons I wanted to break up." I was shocked. I asked her why she had never mentioned this to me, and she responded, "I was too embarrassed to say anything." Years later when I wrote my video, *Intimacy and Sexual Ecstasy,*

I included a communication game where couples specifically share what they like and don't like about their partner's intimate behavior. To this day, I get a lot of letters from couples who tell me sharing that information changed not only their sex life, but the whole way they feel about each other.

3) *What about our making love do you most enjoy?*

4) *What about our making love do you least enjoy?*

5) *What are five things you really like to do with me?*

6) *What are a couple of things I do that really annoy you?*

7) *What have you always dreamed of doing together?*

Questions to Ask *Yourself* to Help Keep Your Love Alive:

1) *What sincere compliment could I give my partner today?*

2) *What act of love or kindness could I do for my partner this week?*

3) *What problems are we having in our relationship that we're not talking about? When and how would be a good way to talk about such things?*

4) *What prevents us from being even more loving or intimate with each other? How might we remove those blocks?*

In my counseling work, I notice that a lot of couples come home completely drained from stressful jobs and then fail to spend any quality time with their partners. Instead, they complain about their day. As this habit gets established, their love slowly fades away. To counteract this tendency, I suggest that couples spend quality time together at least twice per week. During these nights, no complaints or nagging are allowed. In fact, before seeing each other, both partners have to go through a meditation in which they focus on what they love about each other. Couples tell me this little exercise sets the mood for a much more loving night together.

5) *What do I really love and appreciate about my partner?* Meditate on what you love about your partner for a few minutes before spending time with him or her.

6) *What is something fun we can do together this week?* Plan it with your partner.

3

Work/Career

It's true hard work never killed anybody,
but I figure, why take the chance?

—Ronald Reagan

Not all that long ago, men spent most of their lives at a single job, while women spent most of their lives as homemakers. The traditional *Ozzie and Harriet* family of the 1950s hardly exists at all anymore. It's been replaced by a culture that changes jobs, careers and marriage partners almost every decade. With the dizzying level of change that is now occurring, it becomes even more critical to adapt to changing work environments as effectively as possible. Asking the right questions can help you make the necessary changes in order to find lasting fulfillment in your career.

For more than a decade, Srully Blotnick has studied self-made millionaires. Mr. Blotnick admits he had expected to find that most people become millionaires through real estate or high-paying corporate jobs. But his research indicated otherwise. After poring over mounds of data, Mr. Blotnick noticed that the people who got rich were those who reported they absolutely loved what they did. No matter what career these people were in, if they possessed a passion for their work, they tended to work harder and with more enthusiasm. This, in turn, led to them eventually reaching the top of their field. And once at the top of their field, they made a lot of money—even if most other people in their line of work were just barely getting by.

If you really enjoy what you do for money, then you really don't work for a living! You will find many questions here that are aimed to help you find a career that's right for you. If you are already set in a job that fits you, there are a list of questions to help make your current job even more enjoyable and prosperous. Finally, you will find questions that help you anticipate changes in your line of work. By anticipating changes, you can better adapt to new situations and thereby become a leader in your field.

Questions to Ask When Searching for the Right Career or Looking for a New One:

1) *If I didn't need money but was required by law to work, what would I do for free?*

2) *What do other people tell me I'm good at?*

3) *How might I be able to make money from that?*

4) *What did I like to do as a young kid? How might I be able to bring that into my current work?*

For several years, I lived in a beat-up 1967 Dodge van. During this period, I made just enough money to get by and spent most of my time meditating. One day during meditation, the still, small voice in my head came through with a very specific message. It said I should produce an educational video on relationships and sexuality. In order to accomplish this task, I discovered there were a few high hurdles I had to overcome. First, I had less than $300 to my name, and yet the video I had in mind was going to take $45,000 to make. Second, I knew nothing about video production, business, marketing products or raising money. To add insult to injury, my girlfriend at the time chimed in that I also knew nothing about sex!

Still, I trusted my intuition and went ahead as best I could. Using books as my guide, I managed to write the video script and get $20,000 in pledges from various investors. At one point I wondered whether this was really a good idea or not, and it was about this time that I couldn't find any other investors. After several weeks of being afraid to go forward with the project, I asked myself, "What would I do if I knew I could not fail?" I decided to commit to the project and I promptly began it, even though I had less than half the money it would take to complete it. The following day, several investors called me out of the blue and offered me an additional $60,000. In the end, I actually had to turn away investors. The video, titled *Intimacy and Sexual Ecstasy*, became the bestselling educational video in America in 1991 and launched my career.

5) *If I knew I could not fail, what might I try to do for work?*

6) *How can I better express my sense of purpose in my career?*

7) *What kind of work would I like to be doing five to 10 years from now? What's my plan for moving in that direction?*

To Make Your Current Job More Enjoyable and/or Prosperous:

1) *How can I make my work environment more enjoyable?*

2) *How can I make even more of a contribution at work?*

3) *What do I most dislike about my current job? How might I be able to change or improve that?*

I used to work at a halfway house for people with schizophrenia. Although I had a master's degree in counseling, the pay was close to minimum wage. I figured I wasn't getting paid enough to have a bad time, so I decided to just have fun when I went to work. I would bring my guitar and sing silly songs with the patients, perform magic tricks, etc. Generally, I had a great time going to work, and the patients all ended up liking me more than the other counselors. Yet one day I apparently crossed the line. As I was singing with several residents, the entire board of directors of the halfway house walked through for a tour. Without missing a beat, my boss introduced me as the newest patient at the house.

4) *How can I bring more creativity into my work environment?*

5) *What would my boss, employees or customers consider to be my strong points on the job? How about my weaknesses?*

6) *How might I improve on my weaknesses?*

7) *What change is likely to happen in my job or my industry in the next few years? How can I prepare for that now so I can be well-positioned when things do change?*

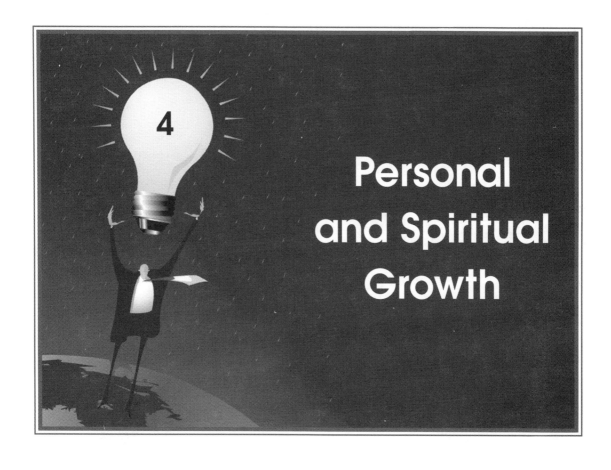

4

Personal
and Spiritual
Growth

*Who is more foolish, the child afraid of the
dark or the adult afraid of the Light?*

—Maurice Freehill

In my previous book, *The Little Book of Big Questions,* I presented over 200 questions to help people focus on the spiritual aspect of their lives. In the numerous letters I received in response to my work, readers often expressed to me how much they were affected by certain questions. Therefore, I've taken a couple of the most practical questions from that book and combined them with some new ones to assist you in evaluating the overall direction of your personal and spiritual life.

In order to know how you're doing in a certain area of life, it's useful to precisely define the goal or target you're aiming for. When it comes to the topic of "spirituality," that precision can be difficult. I witnessed this firsthand when Oprah Winfrey based a show on the questions in my book and all hell broke loose. Everyone in the audience had his or her own idea of what spirituality *really* was and the "right" way to go about spiritual growth. At one point, about 30 people in the audience were all yelling at each other, which led Oprah to exclaim, "I've lost total control of this show!"

So that you'll know what *I'm* talking about when I use the word "spiritual," I'll define it as anything that helps you to feel a deep sense of peace, love, compassion and/or connection to a greater being. When talking about religion or spirituality, people often get lost in differing theologies, and they lose sight of focusing on a deeper experience of love and peace. Therefore, you'll notice that the questions in this chapter avoid theological issues, and instead concentrate on how to have a more satisfying spiritual *experience*. A very cute five-year-old girl on *The Oprah Winfrey Show* was the only person who said something with which everyone could agree. She confidently stated, "I don't know what God is, but I do know where he is. He lives within our own hearts."

As you ask the following questions, tune into the voice or feeling of your own heart. Our soul is always calling to us to become more loving, peaceful and compassionate.

1) *If I were in no way inhibited by fear, how would I be different?*

2) *What personality or character trait would I like to more fully develop? What could I do in order to become more developed in this manner?*

3) *What would I like people to say about me at my funeral? If I died tomorrow, would the people I know say those things, or would they secretly think of me in a different way?*

4) *If I died tomorrow, what would I regret not having done?*

5) *What is my greatest strength? How can I better use this strength to serve myself and others?*

For several years, I lived in a spiritual commune with a teacher whom we all considered to be very wise. About once a week, he would put someone in the "hot seat" and precisely describe the person's shortcomings. The person in the unwelcome position would often elaborately defend him or herself and totally deny the teacher's description. Yet from the vantage point of an observer, I was always amazed at how *accurate* this teacher was in describing the shortcomings of others. Of course, his accuracy tended to fall apart when he was describing *my own* shortcomings. When he put me in the hot seat, I strongly defended and denied his unreasonable and totally untrue accusations. After about a year of this, I finally came to the conclusion that what he said about me must indeed be true, since he was always so insightful about other people. I realized I had somehow hidden my own faults from myself. Once I knew what my biggest shortcomings really were, I found that their grip on me gradually loosened.

6) *What do I consider to be my greatest weakness? What do other people think are my greatest weaknesses? How can I work on or get help in working through these shortcomings?*

7) *When have I felt a strong sense of purpose in my life? How could I increase a sense of purpose in my life right now?*

8) *What helps me to feel a spiritual peace or connection? Am I doing that as often as I would like? If not, how could I make this more of a priority in my life?*

9) *Who is someone I greatly admire? What is it about this person I admire? How can I become more like this person?*

10) *Looking back to who I was five years ago, does it seem like I am growing and changing in beneficial ways? If not, why not?*

11) *In what areas of life would I like to become more developed during the next five years?*

For my book *Bridges to Heaven,* I interviewed 40 well-known spiritual leaders, including Mother Teresa, Wayne Dyer, Marianne Williamson, Bernie Siegel and Ram Dass, asking them how they deepened their relationship with God. I asked each participant the following question: "What cuts you off or lessens your contact with God?" To my surprise, each person reported a very specific and unique way of moving away from God. Several of the people I interviewed said understanding the precise way they move away from God (or their higher self) has been truly instrumental in creating more consistent contact with their spiritual essence. If you have defined exactly what "the wrong direction" is, it's easier to know when you've fallen off "the narrow path" that leads to God.

12) *What is in the way of me having a deeper relationship with and experience of God? (Or a deeper experience of love if you don't believe in God.) How can I overcome or better handle the obstacles to God (or love) that I have in my life?*

13) *What would help me to experience even more love in my life?*

14) *What most helps me hear my own heart and follow its guidance?*

15) *How can I use the gifts I've been given to better serve the highest good for myself and others?*

5

Health

*Health is a state of complete physical,
mental and social well-being, and not merely the
absence of disease or infirmity.*

—Constitution, World Health Organization

In some parts of China, people send money to their doctors only as long as they stay healthy. If and when they get sick, they visit their doctor, but they temporarily *stop* sending them money. After all, the doctor's job is to maintain their health. If they get sick, the prevailing attitude is that the doctor doesn't deserve to be paid. Things are just a tad different in this country. Therefore, if you want to maintain a high degree of health, it's smart to consistently look out for yourself. The questions in this chapter will help you avoid common health problems as well as motivate you toward healthy habits and physical vibrancy.

Many studies have been done to ascertain the reasons why some people are overweight while others are thin. Besides obvious biological differences, researchers have discovered that thin and obese people have different "cognitive processes" with regard to food. In lay terms, this means they ask different questions on the subconscious level. Obese people typically ask themselves the question, "What would taste good right now?" On the other hand, thin people are more likely to ask themselves, "What could I eat that would make my body feel good once I've eaten it?" As you can see, just a slight change in mental focus can have a profound effect on the state of our health.

There's an old adage that says an ounce of prevention is worth a pound of cure. Like most clichés, there's a lot of truth in it. If a little bit of prevention is so powerful, then why don't more people invest their time and money into it? Because most of us don't focus on the long-term effects of our daily health decisions. Questions can help us become aware of the long-term ramifications of what we do every day, and thereby motivate us to take better care of ourselves.

Let the questions that follow guide you toward a state of vibrant health and well-being.

1) *On a scale of one to 10, with 10 being "terrific" and one being "terrible," what is my overall level of health?*

2) *What are a couple of simple things I could do to improve my level of health?*

3) *How much would I like to weigh? What am I willing to do to achieve this ideal weight?*

Recently, an obese woman named Fran came to me for counseling. Fran told me she didn't like being overweight, but she absolutely hated to exercise. I asked her, "What about exercise bothers you?" She reported, "Whenever I work out in the gym, I hate lifting weights, and when I swim, people stare at me because I look so bad in a bathing suit." I asked Fran, "When was the last time your body felt relaxed and filled with energy?" She told me about a recent nature walk she'd been on, and how great she feels after a brisk walk in the nearby mountains. "Why don't you take more nature walks?" was my obvious comeback. Without thinking, Fran responded, "But that would interfere with the time I have to exercise."

I've noticed many people equate exercising with suffering. I've found the opposite is true. Most people won't be consistent with exercise they don't enjoy. When Fran finally realized that walks in the mountains "qualified" as exercise, she began to do her walks four times a week. After three months, she had lost 28 pounds and was even looking forward to more "exercise."

4) *What form of exercise do I most enjoy? How often would I be willing to commit to this form of exercise each week?*

5) *What foods seem to give me indigestion or really zap my level of energy?*

6) *What foods make me feel good after I eat them?*

7) *What am I doing to counter the ongoing stress I have in my life?*

8) *How do I feel about my body?*

9) *Might there be alternative medical and health practices I could try that would improve my level of health?*

10) *Do I eat enough fruits and vegetables? If not, how might I easily include more of them in my diet?*

11) *Do I drink the recommended eight glasses of water each day? If not, how could I make this a habit as soon as possible?*

Several years ago, I hurt my lower back. In an attempt to get well, I sought professional intervention. This turned into a long, frustrating journey in which I visited some 23 different health-care practitioners. All of them thought they knew what my problem was, and they all prescribed a treatment based on their expertise. Medical doctors gave me pills, chiropractors gave me adjustments, physical therapists gave me exercises to do, but none of it seemed to help. Frustrated and ready to give up hope, I complained to a friend about my problem. After hearing me out, she asked me a question that was more helpful than all the advice I had received from the many professionals I had seen: "What have you ever done that has helped your back feel better in the past?" As soon as she asked, I realized that icing my back and doing certain yoga exercises made my back feel better than anything else. Because none of the "experts" suggested such practices, I had stopped doing them. I made a commitment to ice my back and do some yoga every day. Within two weeks my back felt dramatically better.

12) *What have I done in the past that seemed to have a very positive effect on my level of health? How can I do this more frequently in my life? How would that make me feel?*

13) *What is the single worst thing I do for my health? How can I overcome this bad habit?*

14) *Am I taking good care of my teeth by flossing and brushing every day? If not, how could I motivate or remind myself to do this?*

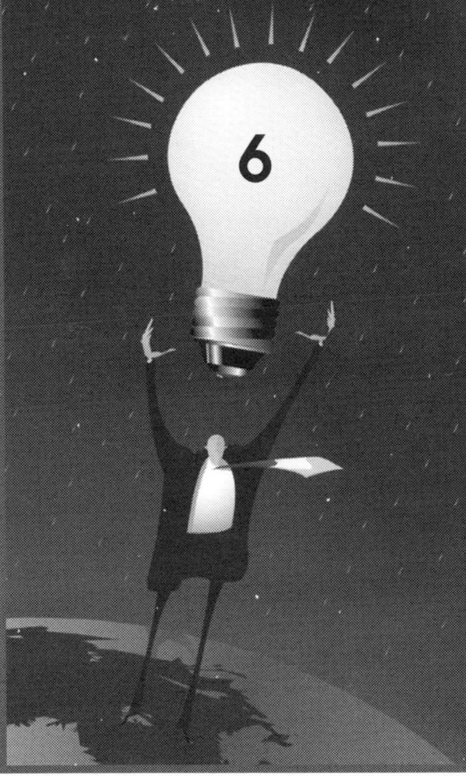

6

Recreation

> *You will soon break the bow if you
> keep it always stretched.*
>
> —Phaedrus

Studies show that Americans have 25 percent less leisure time than they did in 1972. Where has all our time gone? Mostly to increased hours at work. Then, to recover from an exhausting day on the job, the typical American spends over four hours of precious leisure hours watching TV. Commercial TV, of course, is supported by advertisements. In the words of Will Rogers, advertisements exist "to convince you to buy things you don't need with money you don't have." The more we spend, the more we need to work. The cycle perpetuates itself.

Getting off this treadmill is no easy task. Although people typically report feeling worse after they watch TV, a full 90 percent of our free time is spent in front of "the boob tube." Why is that? Well, TV is often the easiest and most convenient form of recreation available. Yet TV can often be depressing (e.g., the news), or downright degrading (e.g., talk shows, violent movies, etc.). Instead of being inspired and refreshed from our discretionary time, many of us end up feeling weary and upset after a night of watching TV. Clearly, we need to seek out new ways to rejuvenate ourselves that are fun, convenient and easy to do.

The following questions are designed to help you explore new ways of having fun, and to motivate you to create quality recreational time on a regular basis. As with all new activities, you'll face some initial resistance when attempting a new sport or hobby. Perhaps you can remember the first time you tried bowling or skiing—it was probably less than spectacular. But if you try something new and stick with it, you'll soon be reaping the rewards of being a more expanded and skillful person. Have fun.

1) *When was the last time I really had a great time? What was I doing?*

2) *What's my favorite leisure time activity? Am I doing it as often as I would like, or as often as would be good for me?*

A common complaint nowadays is that people don't have enough time. Yet the average American ends up watching about 11 years of TV over the course of his or her entire life. That's more than any other activity we partake of, other than sleeping. When you add 10 years on the job (over the course of a lifetime), two years in a car, two years in a bathroom, three years making and eating food, and 25 years sleeping, you're left with very little time to really enjoy yourself. Therefore, it's important to make the most of it!

3) *Do I watch more TV than I would like? If so, how could I limit my TV watching and do something more fun or productive instead?*

4) *What would I like to do for my next vacation? What's the next step I could take in planning it?*

5) *What friends would I like to see more of? What friends would I like to see less of?*

6) *What new recreational activities could I try that might be fun?*

7) *Do I experience enough fun recreational time on a weekly basis? If not, what could I do or what could I eliminate from my life that would give me more time to do the things I truly enjoy?*

I noticed every time I called a psychologist friend of mine, she was either just getting back from a vacation or just about to go on one. So I confronted her. I said, "How can you do that? Doesn't it bother your clients?" She responded, "I simply decided I wanted to take a week off every eight weeks, so that's what I do. My clients have had to learn to adjust to it." Her answer annoyed me. Then I realized I was simply jealous. I made a similar vow to take a week off every eight weeks. Originally it was quite difficult and scary, but I held firm to my commitment. It's been a couple of years now, and I find my bimonthly vacations add immeasurably to my life. Recently, a therapist friend of mine asked me, "Doesn't it bother your clients that you take so much time off?" I told him, "My clients have just had to learn to adjust to it."

8) *How often would I like to take a vacation? What could I do to move in that direction?*

9) *If I had only a few months left to live, would I use my free time differently? If so, exactly how would I use my free time differently?*

10) *If I had no responsibilities and money were no object, what activity or adventure would I like to pursue? Is there a way I can gradually move in the direction of this dream?*

11) *What creative things have I enjoyed doing in the past? Might I enjoy writing something, creating music, painting, or some other form of creativity?*

7

Emotions/ Fulfillment

It is only with the heart one can see rightly;
what is essential is invisible to the eye.

—Antoine de Saint-Exupéry

Modern-day life is filled with so many things to do and take care of that it's easier than ever to lose track of how we actually feel. There's a tendency to put off feeling good until we make more money, find the perfect relationship, send our kids to college or some other external event. There always seems to be a new and perfectly good reason to "put off" feeling good right now. You'll find the questions in this chapter will help you focus on the activities that bring you joy. In addition, these inquiries can help you become aware of and remove the obstacles to joy that you may be experiencing.

At their core, human beings are really simple. Everything we do is ultimately based on our desire to avoid pain and/or our desire to gain pleasure. For example, you bought this book in order to better handle some challenges (avoid pain), or to be entertained (gain pleasure). Unfortunately, many people find that the habitual ways they try to avoid pain or gain pleasure don't work very well. Avoiding the pain of loneliness by becoming drunk does not really end the loneliness—and it creates quite a hangover the next day. When we feel bad, the right question can guide us to handle our pain or create the pleasure we seek in a responsible and effective manner.

In order to avoid pain, people use three major psychological defenses that act to hide the reality of things in their lives. The most common defense is blame. By blaming others for our difficulties, we allow ourselves to feel self-righteous, and we don't have to see how we're responsible for what's going on. The second defense is denial. If we deny that there even *is* a problem, then we don't have to do anything to change. And lastly, there is the defense of seeking constant distraction from the troubling feelings and situations in our life. Each of these defenses helps us put off feeling immediate pain, but the long-term effects can be devastating. When we don't handle a problem when it's small, it gets bigger—until we simply can't hide from it any longer. Some of the questions in this chapter can help you recognize your defenses, and will encourage you to handle the problems they cover before they turn into monsters.

1) *On a scale of one to 10, how happy am I at this point in my life?*

2) *What's my most frequently encountered negative emotion? How might I be able to deal with this feeling, or the situations that lead to it, more effectively?*

A mentor of mine once told me that in order to become a truly fulfilled human being, I would need to know about the "mosquito principle." He said the mosquito principle is the experience of going to Yosemite National Park on a beautiful spring day. You are with people you love, the scenery is gorgeous, and everything is as it should be. As you sit down for a gourmet dinner, a mosquito begins buzzing around your head. Its relentless buzz irritates you to the point that it becomes impossible to enjoy your meal, the scenery or the people you're with.

According to my mentor, the mosquito principle is a reminder that your life is only as good as the very worst thing in your life. That's the thing that gets your attention. Therefore, to become more fulfilled, it's necessary that we always try to improve the worst thing in our life rather than the best. In the mosquito analogy, improving the taste of the dinner wouldn't help much, but getting rid of the mosquito would make a world of difference.

3) *What area of my life feels the worst right now? What am I doing wrong in that area?*

4) *What's my excuse for not doing more of the activities that enliven me? How can I overcome that excuse?*

5) *What are at least five things that bring me down? How can I create my life in a way that I do these things less frequently?*

6) *In what area of my life am I playing a victim by blaming someone or something? How might I be able to take responsibility for what's going on and reclaim my power?*

7) *In what area of my life am I trying to deny or distract myself from an unpleasant reality? What feelings am I afraid of facing? How can I face this situation or these feelings in a small way—so I don't feel overwhelmed?*

To Feel Better:

Have you ever noticed that your mind tends to focus on what's wrong with others, yourself and your life much more than on what's good about others or yourself? Have you ever wondered why that's the case? Fifty thousand years ago, the folks who saw people from a strange tribe and thought, *Oh, I bet they're very friendly,* were often clubbed to death. They didn't pass down their "focus-on-the-positive" genes. On the other hand, the cave men and women who immediately thought, *I bet they're killers,* ran away and got to pass down their paranoid thinking to their children. We, for better or worse, are the descendants of hundreds of generations of paranoid, worried, anxious survivors. We've managed to survive, but in order to thrive, we now need to focus on the positive things in ourselves and others.

You'll notice the following questions are designed to steer your mind in a positive direction. Instead of just intellectually answering these questions, allow yourself to be fully engulfed by the feelings they bring up. Give yourself time to meditate on the experiences they point to. This will take some energy and practice, but it's well worth the effort.

1) *What am I looking forward to?* (Focus on feeling excited about this activity.)

2) *What successes have I had recently?* (See if you can feel proud of yourself.)

3) *What do I or could I appreciate about myself?*

4) *What accomplishment could I feel proud of?*

I had a client who came to me for counseling, complaining of depression. He had been depressed for a while, and he couldn't figure out why. He remarked, "I have a nice house, a secure job and a good family, but I still feel down all the time." I suggested he make two lists. In the first list, I had him write down everything he felt he "had to" do in his life—but didn't really like doing. Next, I had him jot down a list of all the things he'd ever done that had led to a feeling of excitement and energy in his life. The two lists told the whole story. The first list of "have to" items was the life he was currently living. He felt he had to do all these things to be a good person, but they were bringing him no real joy. The second list of "want to" activities were not in his life at all. I told him he simply needed to do more items from the second list and fewer activities from the first list. As he did this, his depression went away.

5) *What are at least five things that bring me a true sense of joy or really enliven me?*

6) *Who is someone I really appreciate or love? What do I like so much about them?* (Meditate on *feeling* your affection for them. If it's appropriate, tell them what you like about them.)

7) *What could I feel grateful for in my life?* (Allow yourself to be filled with the feeling of gratitude.)

8

Problems

All thorns have roses.

—Father David Carriere

We all have problems. Yet some people thrive and grow stronger as they tackle the difficulties in their life, while others grow resentful and weak. Why is it that two people can have such different reactions to the exact same problem?

How we react to a problem is determined by the meaning we give to it. And, of course, the easiest way to change what we make something mean is by asking a new question. The questions in this chapter will help you focus on the hidden opportunity or "gift" in any situation in your life. Although we've all heard that problems can be great growth opportunities, when a problem falls on us, it usually does not feel like a gift. It usually feels like a bus just landed on our shoulders. The next time you bear the burden of a bus (or even a mini-van), turn to these questions.

I tell my counseling clients that the fastest way to become a stronger person is to tackle major problems. When we want to grow physically stronger, we practice lifting an increasing amount of weight. When we "lift" or handle big problems *correctly,* we grow stronger in our compassion, love and courage. The key word here is "correctly." If we lift weights incorrectly, we don't become stronger. In fact, a strained body just makes us more sore. In the same way, if we handle our problems poorly, we become weaker. Yet when we face challenges from an empowered state of mind, our actions are much more effective, and we grow psychological "muscles."

When most people are faced with a difficult problem, they immediately experience a feeling of being overwhelmed. That's why the questions that follow are so important. They are designed to empower you before you become buried by negative thoughts and feelings. Even if you don't want to answer them, force yourself. Within a few moments, they will guide you to a better attitude. Once armed with a good attitude and a little perspective, you'll be well equipped to handle whatever life dishes your way.

1) *In one or two sentences, what's bothering me?*

2) *What are my feelings about it?*

I once wrote a poem based on an ancient Sufi story about how we are often too quick to judge what events mean in our lives. It's called "The Old Man":

Once long ago there lived an old man. He had no money, he had no plan.

All that he had was a horse oh so grand, and he and his horse lived off of the land.

The King offered riches for this horse so fine. "I'll give you my money if you make your horse mine."

But the old man said, "My horse won't be sold. He lives free with me, he lives free and bold."

Then one day, the horse was plain gone. "The horse has been stolen," the townsfolk cried on.

The old man said, "Friends, don't look so sad. Though the horse is gone, that may not be bad."

"You foolish old man, look what you've done. You had a fine horse, and now you have none.

"A curse it is and a curse it'll be. You shouldn't have let your horse wander free."

The horse soon returned with others by its side. There were 12 now of beauty and pride.

The townsfolk said, "Old man, you were right. You're blessed to have horses of unearthly delight."

"I have now 12 horses, yes, that is true. But that doesn't mean I'm blessed with them too.

"It's too soon to judge, who knows what will be? Try not to make stories from the little you see."

As it came to pass, the man's only son tried riding a horse one day just for fun.

Yet he broke both his legs while playing this game, and the townsfolk cried out, "Oh what a shame!"

The old man said, "Friends, don't speak so soon. You hear just one note, but you sing a whole tune.

"Who's to say what the future may hold? My son's legs are broken, but the future untold."

Soon there was war, and the young men of town were all sent to fight and all were shot down.

But the old man's son was saved from this plight. Since he had broken legs, he was not forced to fight.

And the townsfolk cried out, "Again you were right." But the old man replied, "Have you no sight?

"Only God knows what is and will be. To live and let live is to live and be free. . . ."

3) *What am I making this problem mean about myself or about what will happen in the future?*

4) *What else could this mean about myself or about what will happen in the future?*

5) *What could even be good about this situation or problem?*

6) *What attitude or feeling would be helpful to have while dealing with this problem?*

When clients come to see me for therapy, they are often faced with difficult decisions. Deciding such things as whether to divorce, have kids or move to a new city can be extremely difficult. Yet what makes such decisions even harder is our failure to gather all the useful information that would likely lead to a good decision. I tell clients faced with major decisions to try different "experiments" to find out new and useful information about each of their choices. For example, a couple contemplating divorce might try a two-month experiment of living in separate places. A person contemplating a move to a new city might try living in that city for a week and check out the job market. A couple considering having kids might try a week-long experiment of looking after someone else's children. By doing such short-term experiments, new information is gathered that often makes the "right" choice seem quite obvious.

7) *Is there any additional information that would be helpful to have before trying to solve this problem? What "experiment" might I set up to gather more information about my various choices?*

8) Take three deep breaths and try to let go of your feelings about the problem. From what you know now, ask yourself, *"What are simple steps I can take that might help me to solve or better resolve this problem?"* Write all ideas down, including ideas that might be ridiculous.

9) From the above list of steps, what order of actions would be best to take in trying to effectively deal with this problem?

9

Self-
Psychotherapy

> *The gods help them that help themselves.*
>
> —Aesop

What do you think should be the goals of psychotherapy? This is a question I frequently ask my counseling clients. The more we know exactly what we want from an experience, the more likely we'll be able to find it. I've noticed patients typically want to get out of their pain as soon as possible, while spending as little money as possible. On the other hand, psychotherapists, psychologists and psychiatrists have a vested interest in having their patients not get better so quickly. Therein lies the rub. Research shows that the length of time spent in therapy is not nearly the biggest factor that leads to healing. According to numerous studies, success in therapy is largely determined by the attitude of the patient. If a patient has an empowering attitude, good results are practically assured. If a patient has a passive or hopeless attitude, seemingly no length of therapy will be of much help. Since *self*-psychotherapy, by definition, requires the "patient's" active participation in the healing process, it can be surprisingly effective.

In all fairness, I should point out that self-psychotherapy cannot always replace traditional therapy. The relationship between a patient and a therapist is one of the healing aspects of therapy, and cannot be duplicated by a series of questions. Nevertheless, many of the other goals of therapy can indeed be accomplished through the right list of questions. I believe there are three primary goals of successful therapy. First, to get a more objective perspective on what is happening in one's life, and why. Second, to be able to recognize one's ineffective behavior and communication, and accept responsibility for them. And lastly, armed with increased awareness, to be guided toward choosing effective behavior instead. The questions that follow will help you achieve each of these aims.

1) *What is a current concern I have in my life?*

2) *What feelings does this situation bring up for me?*

3) *Can I remember the first time I ever felt this feeling? What was happening then? How is the current situation in my life like the first time I remember having this feeling? How is it different?*

I used to go to great lengths to avoid conflict in my intimate relationships. The truth was, I was terrified of having my partner be angry with me. This fear was interfering with my ability to be intimate and honest with my partner. While in therapy, my counselor asked me the series of questions above. From these questions, I realized that when people were angry at me, it reminded me of when my parents would argue. By the time my parents finally divorced when I was five, I had interpreted their hostility as being my fault, and thought I would be abandoned by both of them. At the time, these feelings were overwhelming. I realized that the occasional anger directed toward me now by my partner brought up these powerful feelings again. Once I was able to see this, I became less afraid. I would reassure myself by thinking, "The anger this person feels toward me will soon pass. Soon, we will work through this and we will feel intimate once again." I am no longer so afraid when people I love are upset at me. I can more easily be myself, and know that I won't be abandoned just because my partner is temporarily upset.

4) *What could I say to myself to help me feel more comfortable with the feelings I'm currently experiencing?*

5) *If I had a magic wand and could make the situation any way I want it to be, how would it be different?*

6) *Is this problem similar to past situations I've had before? If so, how?*

As I mentioned in chapter 7, blame is a powerful defense mechanism that shields us from seeing our own mistakes and shortcomings. The problem is, when we fail to see how we are responsible for what happens to us, we can make the same mistakes over and over again. I encourage all my clients to answer the questions that follow in as much detail as possible. The resistance to these questions is nothing short of monumental. Yet, their importance cannot be overstated. When we can clearly see our own shortcomings, it allows us to avoid falling into the same potholes again and again. It also alerts us to problem areas we are likely to experience—and hopefully avoid through the preventive power of awareness. The following questions are not designed to make you feel guilty or bad. Like a caring friend, they're intended to help you avoid or sidestep future difficulties. Give them your best shot.

7) *How might I be (at least partly) responsible for what's happening now? Or, what shortcomings in myself helped create the current situation or difficulty I'm experiencing?*

8) *What can I learn about myself from seeing these patterns in my life?*

9) *What could I do differently to avoid future problems like the one I'm currently dealing with?*

10) *What could I honestly communicate to others to tell them how I feel, and possibly make the situation that troubles me feel better?*

10

Personal Goals

> *Whatever you can do, or dream you can,*
> *begin it. Boldness has genius, power,*
> *and magic in it. Begin it now.*
>
> —Goethe

Setting goals is one of the most powerful ways to create the life you really want. In 1953, a famous study involving the power of goals began at Yale University. Researchers asked the entire Yale graduating class how many of them had written down any goals for their life. Three percent said they had. Twenty years later, the researchers surveyed the entire class again, looking to see if there were any differences between those who had written down goals and those who hadn't. The 3 percent who had written down goals reported they were happier, in better health, and had a lower incidence of divorce than the students who had not set goals. In addition, the 3 percent who had written down goals in 1953 were, in 1973, worth more monetarily than the other 97 percent *combined!* Writing down what you want in life is an incredibly powerful way to manifest your desires.

I teach a goal-setting class at the local city college and in workshops around the country. Although most people have heard of the importance of setting goals, very few people really do it effectively. To me, a goal is a personal dream you have for yourself, written down on paper, with a deadline attached to it. If it's not written down or does not have a deadline attached to it, it's just a nice idea. A goal can be anything that's important to you, from making a million dollars to attaining a high degree of love or inner peace in your life. In addition, a goal must be measurable, so that you can monitor your progress and know when you've succeeded.

In my workshops, I teach that there are two types of goals: outer goals and inner goals. Outer goals are anything that can be easily measured: making money, creating a new job, taking a vacation, buying a house, etc. Inner goals would include things that are much harder to measure. Examples of inner goals are having more peace, love, or compassion in your life, becoming angry less often, or making more friends. In order to monitor the progress one makes on inner goals, I suggest people come up with an "internal measuring scale." Once a week, you can ask yourself, "On a scale of one to 10, how am I doing on my inner goal?" Then, just get an intuitive sense of how you're doing. While this method isn't perfect, it's a lot better than nothing.

The questions that follow will help successfully guide you through the goal-setting process. Start off with just one goal at a time. Once you've had some success, feel free to add other goals. And remember, pen and paper are needed for these questions. If it's not on paper, it's not really a goal. Although writing your answers to these questions takes some effort, the rewards you'll reap will be well worth it.

1) *What are a few things I would like to have in my life? What's really important to me?*

2) From the list of items you made from the first question, choose one to work on for now. Ask yourself, *In a sentence or two, what is a goal I'd like to achieve?*

3) *By when would I like to achieve it?*

One of the benefits of teaching a class on achieving goals is the feedback I sometimes receive from grateful students. Recently a former student of my class, Otto, spotted me on the street while walking his dog. I asked him how he was doing, and he shared with me a tale of woe. He reminded me that he had taken my class the previous year and had set the goal "to be living with Sally one year from now." Sally was Otto's girlfriend, who lived in a different state. They both hoped to work through the logistics of a long-distance relationship and find a suitable home to share.

In my goals class, I frequently caution the students to be extremely precise with the exact goal they want to achieve. I warn them that a failure to be precise can have unwanted consequences. Otto confessed to me that he felt he hadn't been precise enough with his goal "to be living with Sally a year from now." He stated that he and his girlfriend still lived in different states. But, he sheepishly admitted, "that goal stuff definitely does work. Last week I moved into a really nice house with a roommate who owns this very cute dog". The dog's name, of course, is Sally.

4) *How will I know when I've achieved this goal? What are my specific criteria of success?* (For inner goals rate on a one-to-10 scale where you are at right now. Then decide where you want to be on the one-to-10 scale at the deadline you've set for the completion of your goal. For example: *Right now I'm at a level five of inner peace. In three months I'd like to be at level seven.)*

5) *Why is this goal so important to achieve?* (Write down as many reasons as you can think of as to why this goal is important, and how accomplishing it will greatly improve the quality of your life.)

6) *Whom do I know who has already achieved a similar goal? How can I get information about how they went about it?* (Many experts have written books on their area of expertise. Whenever possible, follow the advice of people who have already accomplished what you would like to achieve.)

7) *What are six or more small steps I could take to move forward toward achieving this goal?*

8) *What steps would be best to do first, second, third, etc.?* Write down all the steps you can think of in a logical order.

When I began my book *Bridges to Heaven,* I knew I would face many obstacles. Interviewing well-known people ranging from Mother Teresa to Kenny Loggins is difficult to do. Such people are very busy. Besides, I couldn't offer them any money for their time and help. When I considered the obstacles before me, I created a list of ways I might be able to overcome these challenges. I decided I would start with lesser-known people and work my way up to better-known people. With each new person I interviewed, I had more credibility to enlist people like Marianne Williamson or Wayne Dyer. In addition, I decided to approach people consistently, week after week. After about a dozen letters to the spiritual teacher Ram Dass, he finally called me. He said, "Since I get so many requests, I usually don't do interviews like this any more. But no one has ever had the persistence you've had. I decided to call to see if you're on a mission from God, or if you're just a lunatic." When I convinced him I was not a lunatic, he gave me the interview. Once he came aboard, many other well-known spiritual leaders soon followed. My plan for getting around the obstacles had worked.

9) *What obstacles do I think I'll encounter along the way? How do I plan to overcome these obstacles?*

10) *How can I make sure I stay consistently motivated to achieve this goal?* (See chapter 14 for a powerful motivation technique.)

11

Family
and
Friends

As the family goes, so goes the nation and so goes the whole world in which we live.

—Pope John Paul II

Nowadays, it's common to hear concerns about the country's moral decline. Everyone from politicians to preachers warns of the problems of family meltdown. The news media are often portrayed as the villains, and we as the helpless victims. It's true that modern-day society can make maintaining strong family and friendship ties harder than ever, but ultimately it's our own choice what we do with our lives. We can give the bulk of our time and energy to TV, work and a host of other things, or we can make caring relationships central to our life.

In recent years, many bestselling books have appeared about people who have had a near-death experience. It is popularly known that when people are clinically dead, they often go through a "tunnel of light," or look down on their body from above. Yet most people aren't aware that almost everyone who has had a near-death experience reports being asked a single question. The question always seems to be the same, no matter who the dying person is or where the person is from. The question is, "What have you learned about being able to love?" It's interesting that almost all religious and spiritual systems make love the central focus of their teachings. To be better prepared for this "test question" at the end of our lives, it's a good idea to "study" for it now. An important way we can learn about love is through the relationships we develop and foster with family and friends. Ultimately, it's the little kindnesses we do for each other, day after day, that determine the quality of love we have in our lives.

Although we all have good intentions, it's easier than ever to get sidetracked from what we truly desire. The questions that follow will help you plan and create the family and friendship ties that really make life worth living. Most worthwhile things don't just magically happen without our conscious planning. By answering these questions, you'll be well on your way to creating and maintaining the type of family and friends you've always wanted.

1) *If I had a month left to live, what would I want to say to each of my family members and closest friends?*

2) *What prevents me from saying those things now?*

3) *Which family member do I find the most challenging to be around?*

I had a client who had spent several years in an ugly battle with his younger brother. In fact, they had spent the previous year refusing to speak to each other. In therapy, it was obvious he still cared for his younger brother, so I suggested he swallow his pride and invite him out to lunch. For this lunch, my client even bought his younger brother a gift. The brothers were able to put aside their past differences, and it ends up they experienced a wonderful "reunion." Four days later, the younger brother was killed in an auto accident by a drunk driver. With tears in his eyes, my client thanked me that I had encouraged him to contact his brother before he died. Although deeply saddened by the unexpected death, he knew he had been freed from experiencing a life time of guilt and regrets.

4) *Is there anything I could say or do that might make it easier for me to be around a family member I've found difficult to deal with in the past?*

5) *Whom do I consider to be my closest friend? What about them do I really like?*

6) *Have I told this special friend how much I value and appreciate them? If not, why not?*

7) *What activity could I do with friends that would be fun to do and help bring us closer together?*

8) *What kind gesture could I make to a family member or friend this week?*

Kids

If You Don't Have Kids Yet:

1) *If I choose to have kids, how many would I like to have?*

2) *How old would I like to be when I have each of them?*

3) *Do I always make sure a birth control method is used if I'm having sex without the intention of having kids? If not, why not?*

In the high school I went to, they had an innovative program to help curb teen pregnancy. They had women who had become pregnant in their teens talk to us about the details of raising an unexpected child. For homework, we were given the assignment of taking care of a 20-pound bag of flour, watching it and carrying it around with us every minute of the day. At night, we were supposed to wake up at 3:00 A.M. and hold our bag of flour for 10 minutes—so it could go back to "sleep." Before meals, we would take five minutes and pretend to feed our bag of flour. It may seem funny, but this little exercise had a profound effect on us.

I'm still friends with several of the people who took that class. So far, none of us have had kids yet.

4) *Have I talked to people who have kids about the life style changes that occur when having a child?*

5) *Have I talked with my partner about his or her expectations of who will change the baby's diapers, feed the baby in the middle of the night and all the other responsibilities of having a child?*

6) *Have I talked to my partner about how our relationship is likely to change once we have a child?*

If You Already Have Kids:

1) *When was the last time I told my kids how much I love them?*

I once heard there was a child psychologist who wrote a book called, *The 10 Commandments for Raising a Child.* Over a couple of years, the book became a bestseller. During this time, the psychologist got married and had his first child. When his publisher requested he do a second edition to the book, he decided to rename it *The 10 Guidelines for Raising a Child.* As the years passed, the psychologist and his wife had two more children, and the new edition of his book continued to do very well. When his publisher finally requested a third edition to the book, the psychologist and father of three renamed the book *10 Things You Might Want to Try When Raising a Child.*

2) *What is the biggest problem I have in my relationship with my kids? What could I do differently that might help lessen or resolve this problem?*

3) *What do I need to communicate to my mate (or ex-mate) in order to have more harmony in how we both raise our child?*

4) *How might I go about helping to raise my child's level of self-esteem?*

5) *Do my children feel like I really listen to them? Do I feel like they really listen to me?* If not, ask them, "What could we do differently so that both of us feel better listened to?"

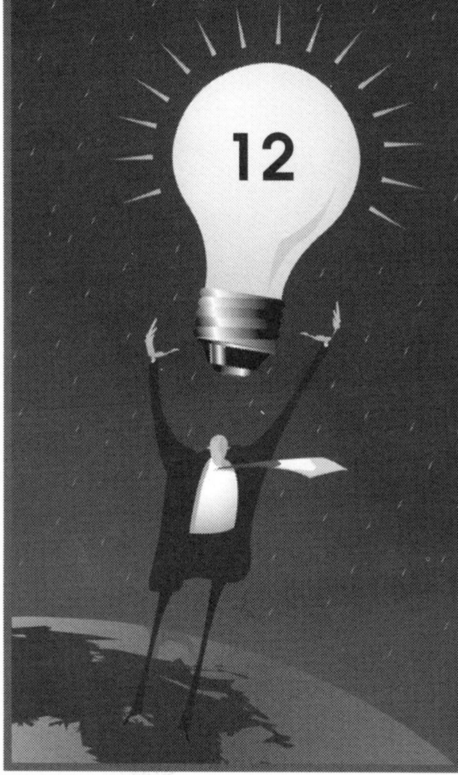

12

Money

> *There is a gigantic difference between earning
> a great deal of money and being rich.*
>
> —Marlene Dietrich

For several years, I've taught a workshop called "From Money Madness to Money Magic." In it, I teach people how to make more money with less effort, while doing what they enjoy. For most of us, doing work that's enjoyable and highly profitable seems like an impossible dream. Yet in the workshops I lead, I teach that "money magic" is a learnable skill that involves three primary steps. First, you must have a passionate reason *why* you want to make a lot of money. A desire for a nicer car or a need to pay your bills is not a truly passionate reason. Ultimately, what's most important to us is our desire for more peace, love, joy and contribution. Therefore, in order to really want more money, you must have a plan for how money can significantly improve the quality of your life.

People who say "money can't buy you happiness" clearly don't know how to "shop" properly. Money can buy you more than just material goods. It can also buy you therapy if you've lost your way, soothing vacations if you're stressed out, or quality time and experiences with the people you love. Once you know how money can really add to the quality of your life, a second step toward abundance is to get past all the psychological obstacles to making money. To make a lot of money, you must become skillful in taking risks, staying motivated and facing the fear of failure or rejection. Without the help of the right questions to prod us along, we can easily be stopped by such psychological roadblocks.

The third thing I teach in my Money Magic seminars is the ability to master financial investment and marketing strategies. If you build a better mousetrap, no one will really care—unless you know how to market it properly. Likewise, if you make a lot of money and then invest it poorly, you'll be back at square one.

The questions that follow are largely focused on guiding you through the three stages of creating Money Magic I just mentioned. Once you know how money could improve the quality of your life, and you've steered past the psychological obstacles, you'll find manifesting money a lot easier and more fulfilling than ever before. Then your only problem will be figuring out what to do with all the extra dough. Some problems are worth having.

1) *How could I use an extra $5,000 to improve the quality of my life? How about an extra $50,000?* (Be as specific as possible.)

2) *What charities or causes would I like to support if I had more money?*

3) *If I were not inhibited by the fear of failure or rejection, what could I do to make more money?*

4) *What did my parents teach me, directly or indirectly, about money as I was growing up? Is there a new way of looking at money that would be more beneficial to me?*

When I was living in my 1967 Dodge van, I had a job teaching a course at the local city college that made me about $250 a month. Since I had few expenses living in a van, I was able to save about $75 a month. Although I was making very little money, I felt grateful for having a place to sleep and plenty of money for food and entertainment. One day, as I was sitting in the sauna at the gym I belonged to, a man named Harry began talking to me about the stresses in his life, especially his money situation. He complained that he just couldn't make ends meet on $40,000 anymore. To me, this seemed like an enormous amount of money, but I tried to be understanding. I said reassuring words to him about how the cost of living is high in Southern California. Then Harry said something that made me realize a person can feel poor on any income level. He despondently stated, "You know, you just *can't* get by in this town on $40,000 *a month.*"

5) *What stops me from appreciating the money I have in my life? How can I let go of that and immediately tune into feeling grateful for all the money and riches I already have?*

6) *Do I have a plan for making extra money? Have I shared my plan with others to see if it's realistic?*

7) If you have kids: *Am I planning on helping them through college? If so, what would be a realistic savings plan?*

8) *How could I give some money away to people or causes I believe in that would make me and others feel good?*

9) If you are married: *Do I have differences of opinion with my mate over how to control the money? If so, what can we do differently that might help resolve such issues?*

10) *What could I do differently to get a better handle on my financial situation?*

I had a client who was a tree trimmer and who frequently complained he didn't make enough money. I asked him, "On average, how much money do you make for each job you do?" It ends up he made about $1,000 per job, of which virtually all was profit. I also asked him how many referrals he gets for each job he does. He reluctantly offered, "Maybe one referral for every three jobs I do." I excitedly told him, "That means you make about $1,333 profit for each customer who calls you. Why don't you offer every client $300 cash for each referral they give you that ends up becoming a paying customer? That would still mean you'd make $1,000 per customer." To make a long story short, he tried it. Soon he was averaging six referrals per customer, 18 times his previous referral base. In one month his business increased 400 percent; in three months it increased 1,100 percent. Eventually, he hired a manager to handle all the businesss and he took a long-awaited trip around the world. By knowing what each customer was worth to him and using an incentive to get more business, he was able to make more money in one year than he had in the previous 10.

11) *What could I do to market myself more effectively? Would it be possible to give some incentive for referrals, or to do a special project for my boss that would put me in line for a promotion?*

12) *What are at least three creative and fun ways I could make additional income?*

13) *Do I know how to get high yields with my investments? If not, what resource could I use to help me make highly profitable investments?*

13

Grow
Your Own
Questions

I keep six honest serving men, they taught me all I knew;
Their names are What and Why and When and
How and Where and Who.

—Rudyard Kipling

W hen I see clients in my psychotherapy practice, I frequently point out that many of their problems stem from habitually asking themselves harmful or obsolete questions. For example, people who are fearful a lot of the time subconsciously ask themselves the question, "What bad things might happen in this situation?" Since they habitually focus on this question, their brain starts to look for and imagine painful or embarrassing incidents that could happen in the near future. By focusing intently on such a question, they find answers—whether the dangers are real or not.

Based on our early childhood experiences, we all create subconscious questions that filter what we attend to in any given situation. At one time these subconscious questions helped to protect us and make us feel safe. Unfortunately, they are usually no longer necessary or helpful in dealing with our current life situations.

The fact that these questions are subconscious, and therefore outside our conscious awareness, is the bad news. The good news is it's possible to figure out what our obsolete subconscious questions are, and then come up with "antidote questions" that can immediately make us feel better. I'll use a recent client as an example of how this process works. Sarah originally came to me expressing symptoms of depression and stress. She worked about 60 hours a week, came home and took care of her husband and her kids, and almost never allowed any time for herself. I asked myself, "What question must she be asking subconsciously in order for her to create the experience of never having time for herself?" I guessed she must be habitually asking herself, "What else needs to be done?" Indeed, when I mentioned this to Sarah, she responded by saying this question sounded like what she says to herself many times throughout the day.

By asking this question, she is able to seek out and find a continual stream of things to do. The only problem is, such a question leaves no time for fun.

As we explored her childhood, Sarah remembered that her mother used to yell at her whenever she didn't finish all her chores before going out to play. Therefore, she created the question of "What else needs to be done?" to help her avoid the intense yelling of her mother. Yet now, this same question was making her an unwilling slave of constant activity. So I suggested to her an "antidote" question: "What could I do now to take the best possible care of myself?" When Sarah asked this new question throughout the day, she received a variety of answers. Sometimes, getting a specific task done was a way of taking care of herself. Yet frequently, taking care of herself meant asking her husband for help, or taking a short break, or deciding to have some fun instead of continually working.

An easy way to figure out the questions bouncing around in your own subconscious is to reflect on what gives you difficulty in life. What problematic experiences happen to you again and again? What are your most frequent negative emotions? On the pages that follow, I list some common problems and negative feelings that people experience. Beneath each of these conditions, I've listed the subconscious questions that typically lead to these problems or painful conditions. Finally, I provide antidote questions that can help you overcome your habitual tendencies. By focusing on the antidote questions that relate to your problem area, you'll notice profound positive changes in your experience of life. The more you use the appropriate antidote questions, the quicker and more powerful the effect will be.

For each problem, I list several questions that could potentially lead to negative feelings. When you read a question that is similar to one used by your subconscious mind, it may feel "familiar." When you read the antidote questions, you may notice a light bulb going off in your mind at the question that would be most helpful to you. Trust your gut feeling. Go with the questions that feel right for you. When asking your new questions throughout the day, make sure you take the time to truly tune into an answer. Sometimes, a question directs you to *feel* something—rather than just know something intellectually. For example, asking the question "What am I grateful for?" could be answered rationally, but the point of the question is to get in touch with the *feeling* of gratitude. It will take some practice to get good at tuning into the positive feelings alluded to in the antidote questions. It is time well spent.

I. Problem or Negative Tendency:

Feeling bad about yourself; feeling little self-confidence; feeling insecure.

Subconscious questions that create this experience:

1) *Why can't I do anything right?*

2) *Why is everyone else better off than me?*

3) *What's wrong with me?*

4) *How am I likely to blow it in this situation?*

Antidote questions to feel better:

1) *What could I like and appreciate about myself?* (Remember to take the time to really *feel* the answers to these and the following questions.)

2) *What is something I've done successfully recently?*

3) *Who is someone who really appreciates me?*

II. Problem or Negative Tendency:

Feeling continually stressed out; never having enough time; feeling hurried.

Subconscious questions that create this experience:

1) *What else needs to be done?*

2) *What else do I have to do today?*

3) *What terrible thing will happen if I don't complete everything I need to do today?*

Antidote questions to feel better:

1) *What could I do now to take the best possible care of myself?*

2) *What can I do to have fun today?*

3) *If I don't finish everything on my "to do" list, would that be so terrible?*

4) *What could I delegate to others to do so that I can have more time for myself?*

III. Problem or Negative Tendency:

Always feeling down or depressed.

Subconscious questions that create this experience:

1) *What's wrong with the world?*

2) *What's wrong with me?*

3) *Why have I been dealt such a bad deal?*

4) *How will this seemingly positive experience (or person) end up causing me pain?*

5) *What else is wrong in my life?*

Antidote questions to feel better:

1) *What's right with the world?*

2) *What could I feel grateful for?*

3) *What am I already doing successfully?*

4) *What do I appreciate about myself?*

5) *What am I looking forward to?*

IV. Problem or Negative Tendency:

Being quick to anger; raging; being annoyed a lot of the time.

Subconscious questions that create this experience:

1) *How is this person screwing me over?*

2) *How is this person full of crap?*

3) *How is this person doing something totally unfair to me?*

Antidote questions to feel better:

1) *What pain must this person be experiencing in order to act this way?*

2) *How is what they're doing like something I do?*

3) *What could I like or appreciate about this person?*

4) *What expectation do I have for how people should act that I have failed to express clearly?*

5) *Would I rather be right and self-righteous, or would I rather be peaceful and happy?*

V. Problem or Negative Tendency:

Feeling frustrated a lot; feeling other people can't be trusted to do something right; being in a hurry much of the time.

Subconscious questions that create this experience:

1) *Why can't anybody do anything right?*

2) *Why won't they see it my way?*

3) *If it's not done exactly the way I want it, when I want it, what price am I going to have to pay?*

4) *Why do I have to take care of everything myself?*

Antidote questions to feel better:

1) *What is their point of view?*

2) *If things don't go exactly the way I want them to, can I still be okay?*

3) *What is already going the way I want it to?*

4) *How might I express my needs better so that people are more responsive to them?*

5) *Would I rather be right or get the job done as best as possible?*

VI. Problem or Negative Tendency:

Feeling guilty much of the time; feeling ashamed of yourself for past behavior.

Subconscious questions that create this experience:

1) *What's wrong with me?*

2) *What do I need to hide from this person?*

3) *What should I have done?*

4) *Why can't I do anything right?*

Antidote questions to feel better:

1) *What are things I've done that make me like or feel good about myself?*

2) *What good reasons did I have for acting the way I did in the past?*

3) *How can I learn from what I did and make an even better decision next time?*

VII. Problem or Negative Tendency:

Being dissatisfied much of the time; feeling like there's never enough; disappointment.

Subconscious questions that create this experience:

1) *Is this all there is?*

2) *Why isn't this better or more the way I like it?*

3) *What am I missing?*

Antidote questions to feel better:

1) *What could I feel grateful for?*

2) *What do I really like about . . . ?*

3) *What's great about . . . ?*

VIII. Problem or Negative Tendency:

Feeling anxious much of the time; feeling fearful; feeling out of control.

Subconscious questions that create this experience:

1) *What might go wrong?*

2) *What dangerous or embarrassing things might happen?*

3) *What if [some negative situation] happens?*

Antidote questions to feel better:

1) *Could I handle it if things don't go exactly the way I want?*

2) *What can I do to be even better prepared to handle what I'm worrying about?*

3) *What am I proud of in my life?*

4) *Am I worrying unnecessarily about this? Will my worry help?*

Because life is so complex, you may find you have a difficulty that doesn't easily lend itself to the challenges just listed. Therefore, it's useful to know how to tailor-make your *own* questions to meet the unique challenges in your own life. A simple way to do this is to write down your problem in a sentence or two. Then ask yourself, "What questions would help me better deal with this problem?" Write down anything that comes to mind, even if it seems ridiculous. Often, the fourth or fifth question you brainstorm will be the best.

Recently, I realized I had a brand new problem. Several of my closest friends had moved out of town, and I was missing them. Although I still had friends in town, they were more like acquaintances than close friends. So I wrote down on a piece of paper:

PROBLEM: a lack of close friends who live near me.

Then I began brainstorming questions that might help me overcome this challenge. These were my first six questions:

1) *Where and how could I meet new friends?*

2) *How could I maintain a close relationship with my friends who have moved out of town?*

3) *How can I deepen the friendships I already have with people in town?*

4) *Whom would I like a deeper friendship with?*

5) *How can I deepen my out-of-town friendships and the ones I have in town, quickly and easily?*

6) *How much time and energy am I willing to devote per week to having and deepening my friendships?*

Sometimes, a single question from the many you write down will leap up off the page and declare, "I'm the question for you!" Other times, all the questions you write down will seem about equally helpful. In this case, I found all the questions useful, and the answers were rather obvious to me once I was asking the right questions. With the insight I received from asking good questions, I have been able to move toward my goal of deepening friendships. Try this process out for yourself with any problem you currently have. I think you'll be surprised how easily answers appear when the right questions are asked.

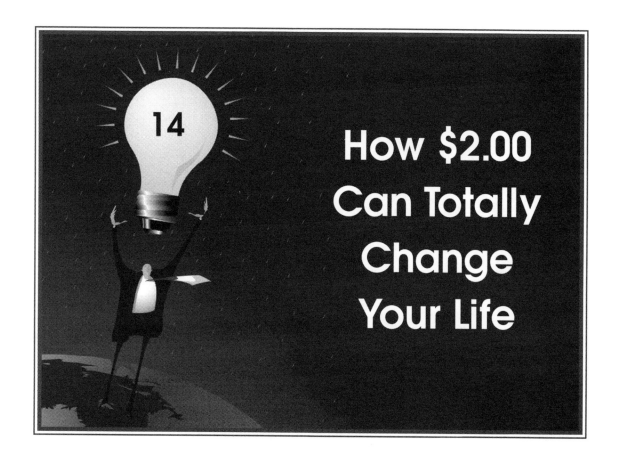

14

How $2.00
Can Totally
Change
Your Life

> *A lot of people know what to do, but*
> *few people do what they know.*
>
> —Anthony Robbins

Even before asking my clients useful questions, many of them already know what they need to do to make their life better. The problem is, they just don't do it. I can relate. I used to have many things I wanted to do, but it seemed I was too lazy or too busy to consistently do them. I wanted to exercise, I wanted to meditate, I wanted to work on my career goals, I wanted to be more loving to my girlfriend. Yet my laziness would soon take over, and these goals would fade into oblivion. So I set out to find a motivational method that would work even for someone as lazy and busy as me. My hope was that the right technique would fire me up to actually do all those behaviors that I knew would make my life better. After several years of trying and then trashing just about every motivational method there is, I created a technique that invariably worked for me. In the last four years I've taught it to hundreds of people, and *everyone* who uses it reports getting *phenomenal* results. I can boldly state that this method will give you the ability to consistently follow through on whatever makes your life happier and healthier.

Before divulging this technique, which I call the I.C.A.N. method, let me give you some background theory as to how and why it works so well. As I mentioned in chapter 7, everything we do is ultimately to avoid pain and/or gain pleasure. The problem is, many of the behaviors that are good for us, such as exercising, are immediately painful to do. Since we're wired to avoid pain, getting ourselves to exercise can be quite a task. Only when we focus on the pain of *not* exercising, such as being out of shape or dying sooner, are we able to get ourselves to act. Unfortunately, this doesn't always work because the pain of not exercising (being out of shape) is not really *immediate*, whereas the pain of exercising is oh so real.

With this pain/pleasure principle in mind, I set out to find a pain I'd be willing to immediately give myself if I failed to do the actions that supported a better life. After much trial and error, I came up with the perfect solution. The acronym I.C.A.N. stands for the Integrity Contract And Nurturance method. Each week I write on a piece of paper a contract such as the following:

I, Jonathan Robinson, agree to do the following actions this week:

1) *I will exercise three times this week for a minimum of one hour each time.*

2) *I will meditate or do some other stress-reducing activity at least four times this week for a minimum of 10 minutes each.*

3) *I will make at least 10 calls this week to promote my latest book.*

4) *I will ask myself the question, "What's a loving thing I can do right now?" at least once a day.*

Once I've written three or four important but hard-to-do behaviors on my "contract," I write the following key words:

"For each item on my contract that I fail to complete by one week from today, I agree to rip up $2.00."

That's it. Ripping up $2.00 is a universal pain—nobody likes to waste money.

In order for this method to create amazing changes in your life, you don't have to have faith in it, you don't have to believe in it, you don't even have to like it. You just need to use it. Once you learn how to use this technique properly, you'll be able to follow through on all those things you used to procrastinate over or avoid. It will change your life.

After you've written the precise actions you plan to do on your contract, sign and date your contract, and set it in a place wher you'll see it every day. Many people find that taping this sheet of paper to their bathroom mirror is a helpful daily reminder. At the end of the week, if there is any item on your contract you failed to complete, take out the appropriate amount of money and rip it to shreds. Don't think of it as a punishment. Think of ripping up money as a way to boost your integrity and the power of giving your word.

Admittedly, tearing up money is not a fun thing to do. I have hundreds of stories of people who have altered the course of their life to avoid ripping up $2.00.

I've used this technique to get people off heroin and cigarettes. I've used this method to get people to exercise consistently so that they could lose weight. I've used this method to help people increase their income 500 percent in one year. It works with lazy people, it works with busy people, it even works for people who are absolutely sure that it won't work for them. If you use it, it *will* work.

Some people worry it might be illegal to rip up money. In order to see if ripping up money was legal, I called the Secret Service. After talking to four employees who didn't know if it was legal or not, I talked to the top guy at the Secret Service. He combed through the appropriate legal book and proclaimed, "It doesn't say anything about ripping up your own money. Therefore, I guess it's okay. I've been here for over 30 years and no one has ever even asked such a question!"

There are several reasons why this method is so effective. First, there is a clear proclamation of what you intend to do, and by when you plan to do it. Normally, people have a lot of lofty *thoughts* about what they could do to improve their life, but these thoughts soon slip away. With the I.C.A.N. method, you'll have a visual reminder of what you're committed to do. Secondly, with this technique, you'll experience immediate pain if you fail to keep your word. Since your brain is always trying to avoid immediate pain, it will do its best to complete what's on the contract.

You might be wondering, Why rip up $2.00? Why not $1.00 or $5.00? Having used this method with countless people over the years, I've seen that $2.00 works the best for most people. When people write down that they'll rip up $5.00 for each incomplete task, when push comes to shove, they often fail to rip up the money. Instead, they make excuses as to why they couldn't finish their contract, or they just blow the whole thing off rather than rip up the money. Basically, their promise to themselves is not worth a full $5.00. On the other hand, if there is only a threat of ripping up $1.00, some people find $1.00 isn't painful enough to keep them motivated. Most people find the threat of ripping up $2.00 enough to get the job done, and if they don't complete their contract, they are willing to rip up the money to avoid breaking a promise they made to themselves.

As far as I'm concerned, it's fine to not complete everything on your contract— as long as you rip up the money for the tasks you don't finish. I've seen that as long as people are willing to rip up money for failing to complete their contract, the method eventually works. Maybe not the first or second week, but by the third week, you'll find your mind screaming at you to complete whatever you wrote down. After a while, the I.C.A.N. method becomes like a trusted friend. You rely on it to help you do all the important things you used to procrastinate over. As an added bonus, this technique helps you to build confidence. You begin to see you can take effective action simply by stating what you're committed to do each week, and then keeping your word.

Joan came to me for counseling, complaining that her life was a big ugly mess. She didn't have the job she wanted, she was without a partner, overweight and totally stressed out. Rather than explore the difficulties of her childhood, I immediately taught her the I.C.A.N. method. She immediately used it to exercise consistently and take warm baths more frequently to relax. Soon she had lost the unwanted pounds she had been carrying, and the baths helped her to be more relaxed and at ease with herself. Joan proceeded to put on her contract simple weekly tasks to find a better job. After six weeks, she found the job she was looking for. It only took three more weeks to meet the man she later married, a fine young man who worked at her new job. In three months of using the I.C.A.N. method, Joan had transformed her life from a mess to a masterpiece. I should point out she wasn't always successful in completing her contract. In three months she missed four items, for a total of $8.00. Yet now she had a job she liked, a man she loved, a body that was hot, and a sense of really liking herself for the first time in years. Not bad for $8.00.

What follows is a step-by-step account of how you can use the I.C.A.N. method each week to solve problems, work on your goals, and create a healthier and happier life.

1) *Do something to quiet your mind. When you feel quiet inside, ask yourself, "What important things could I do this week to create a life of even more inner and outer riches?" Write down whatever ideas you get.*

2) *For the two, three or four best ideas you come up with from #1, create simple measurable tasks you can do within the course of a single week. For example, the inner message to "focus on your relationship" might lead to the action of having a romantic night out with your partner. To increase your business exposure, you could put on your contract the task of giving out your business card to four potential customers.*

3) *Write down on a single sheet of paper all the specific things you plan to do by the end of one week. Then, state that for each item you fail to complete by the end of the week, you will rip up $2.00. Sign and date your contract. Below is an example of how such a contract looks.*

> I, Jonathan, agree to do the following over the course of the next week:
>
> a) Call five potential clients about my new seminar.
>
> b) Meditate for 15 minutes each day.
>
> c) Exercise a minimum of three times, for at least 40 minutes each time.
>
> d) Start a savings account to save money for a vacation to Europe.
>
> For each of the above items I fail to complete by 5:00 P.M. next Thursday, I agree to rip up $2.00.
>
> [current date] [your signature]

4) *Put the contract in a place where you'll see it daily. If you have an appointment book, make sure you write down the exact time you plan to evaluate your contract.* It's important that you schedule this. *If possible, make this appointment exactly one week from the writing of the contract.*

5) *At the end of the week, evaluate how you did. If you didn't complete any items on your contract,* no matter what your excuse, *tear up the appropriate amount of money. It may take awhile to write contracts that work just right for you. Go through this process again for the upcoming week. Write a new contract that takes into account what worked for you in the previous week and what did not. Feel free to write contracts over and over again that consist of the same tasks. After a few weeks, you'll find you can write highly beneficial contracts in a matter of two or three minutes. If you find you always miss items on your contract, write easier contracts. On the other hand, if you find you always complete everything, put a couple of more difficult items on your list. Have fun.*

In the previous chapters, many questions pointed you to ideas and goals that are important to you. Think of how quickly you could make them a reality if you made progress on them each and every week. After a while, the I.C.A.N. method becomes a fun game you play with yourself. Rather than always putting off the dreams you have, it allows you to act on them right now. People who have the patience to slowly but surely make progress on their goals are the people who succeed in life.

In seminars I lead about the I.C.A.N. technique, I usually get asked very similar questions about this method. Therefore, what follows are the most common questions and their respective answers about this process:

Why is it called the Integrity Contract and Nurturance Method?

For two reasons. First, I wanted an acronym that would be easy to remember and would remind people what this method is for. The words "I can" aptly summarize the idea that whatever your goals are, they can be achieved through this process.

Secondly, I included the words "integrity" and "nurturance" in the method's name to remind people about *how* to properly use this process. This technique is really based on increasing your personal integrity, also known as the power of your word. I like to think that the ripping up of money isn't really a punishment, but rather an "integrity booster shot." By keeping to your contract, you increase your level of integrity and thereby achieve greater personal power.

The word "nurturance" is used to signify that this method aims to nurture your dreams—not to make you feel guilty. Occasionally, people use the I.C.A.N. process to overwhelm themselves and make their life unnecessarily difficult. If that's your experience with this process, then you're using it incorrectly. The goal of this method is to nurture the deepest desires you have for yourself and your life. By doing small tasks each week that help you to be more successful in life, you can make steady progress without feeling overwhelmed with too much to do.

I find I'm already too busy in my life. How can I add additional stuff without feeling even more burdened?

The contracting process requires that you decide what's *most important* to do each week. Typically, people get caught up in doing a lot of easy but rather trivial stuff—and never spend time working toward what's really most important in their life. The I.C.A.N. method can give you the power to always get the important stuff done. Sometimes, this will require you to leave some relatively unimportant things undone. Part of what makes this process so powerful is its requirement that you consciously *prioritize* the tasks in your life. It puts you firmly in control. If you feel like you're doing too much, then you are even *more* in need of prioritizing the tasks in your life. No matter how busy you are, you always have time for what's *really* important. The I.C.A.N. process will simply have *you* decide what's important, rather than having the habits you've developed in the past determine your future.

What do I do if an emergency comes up and I'm not able to do the tasks on my contract?

This is a tough question. I *used* to tell people, if any emergency comes up, just forget about your contract for that week. Then I noticed an interesting phenomenon: People were having emergencies on a weekly basis! When I'd ask what their emergency was, occasionally I'd hear excuses like, "My mom called and upset me," or "I stubbed my toe." I even noticed that I was beginning to make slimy rationalizations to invalidate my own contracts. Therefore, I now suggest that people specify the terms by which a contract can be made invalid.

In my own case, at the bottom of my weekly contract I state: This contract is invalid only under the following conditions:

- I am too sick to work for more than one day.
- I have to attend a loved one's funeral.
- I have an injury or illness that requires hospitalization.

As you can see, I give myself little leeway to excuse myself from my contracts. I think it's best like this. I suggest you come up with specific conditions for which your contracts would be made invalid. Write them down. Don't underestimate how slippery your mind will be in trying to avoid ripping up money. If your "emergency" isn't specified beforehand, then ripping up money is in order.

Instead of ripping up money, can I simply give it to a needy person or to a charitable organization instead?

In a word, no. Part of the power behind this method is that it's quite painful to rip up money. You'll do a lot to avoid committing such a wasteful act. Last year, as an experiment, I allowed one group I worked with to give their money away instead of ripping it up. The results were disastrous. The effect of the I.C.A.N. process was diluted about 80 percent. On the other hand, I have since found that people who have spent about *two years* ripping up money *can* begin giving it to charities without a significant loss of its effectiveness. After two years, it seems that not fulfilling one's promise (as outlined in the contract) is as motivating as what is done with the money. Trust me on this one. For at least the first two years of using this method, rip up the money if you don't complete the items on your contract.

If you simply can't get yourself to rip up $2.00 for each broken agreement, then consider allowing yourself to rip up $1.00 for missed contractual items. Some people have even successfully made contracts that state they'll throw away a mere $.25 if they fail to complete an item on their contract. I suggest you start out with ripping up $2.00 for each missed agreement, but after a couple of weeks, feel free to raise or lower that amount if you feel it would better suit your needs. If you find you're starting to make excuses for why you're not completing your agreements, you're either making your contract too difficult or the amount you're ripping up is too high for you. Conversely, if you easily rip up money, you might try raising the price tag on each broken agreement to $5.00.

What items are good to put on a contract, and what is better left off?

If you ordinarily make five sales calls a week, there's no need to put that down on a contract. After all, you're already doing it. But if there's something you're not doing, but you know it would benefit your life and/or well-being, then a contract will be of great help to you. Also, contracts are useful for breaking large goals into small tasks easily accomplished within a week.

If you have a goal that is very large, then it doesn't belong on a contract. An example of this would be the goal of selling your house. Putting such a large goal on a weekly contract would simply add unnecessary pressure. Instead, ask yourself, "How could I break this into several smaller steps?" Tasks such as "talk to three Realtors" and "call for an appraisal" would fit well on a contract and be useful to move you in the direction of selling your house.

Why are contracts always for one week? Why not for one day or one month?

Experience has shown me that a single week works best. We tend to think in week-long increments, divided up between five days of work and a two-day weekend. When people have to make contracts for a longer period of time, the result has been less focus and more broken agreements. If you try to make contracts for less than a week's time, you'll spend all your time writing contracts— instead of taking beneficial action.

How many items should I put on the contract?

I suggest people begin with no more than two or three tasks on each weekly contract. Then, once you get used to that, feel free to slowly add additional items. Currently, I put about 15 tasks on my weekly contract, but I've been doing this for over five years. It's important you don't use this process to overwhelm yourself. First build a momentum of successes. Once you have a successful routine of completing whatever is on your contract sheet, you're ready to gradually add more tasks, some of which may be more difficult.

I sometimes forget to evaluate my contract at the end of the week. What can I do to make sure I don't forget?

Several things can be helpful for putting an end to this problem. First, it's important to realize this problem can simply be a creative way of resisting this very powerful process. Since this technique can dramatically alter your life, it's not unusual that some form of resistance will appear—at least initially. But once you've done this method for a month or so, your subconscious mind will notice it really improves your life, and therefore will resist it less.

Many people have found that coming up with a ritualized time for writing and evaluating contracts helps them to be consistent. For example, if you always do this process Sunday night or before work on Monday morning, you'll be less likely to "forget." Secondly, you can add to your contract the caveat that if you fail to evaluate your progress on the specified date, you have to rip up an additional $2.00.

Experience has shown me that the most effective way to be consistent with the I.C.A.N. process is to do it with a friend or mate. When doing this, you simply call or visit each other at the appropriate time each week and tell them how it went.

Having an "accountability partner" is a great way to keep the contract process alive, and has the added advantage of assisting your friend or partner in reaching *his or her* most important goals. *I strongly encourage you to find such a partner.* A five-minute phone call or meeting with your partner once a week is enough to keep the I.C.A.N. method working effectively in your life.

Some people are hesitant to ask someone to be their "accountability partner." But introducing a friend, family member or intimate partner to this process is perhaps the greatest life-changing gift you can give them. Sharing the effect this process has had on your life is a great way to keep your own enthusiasm for the method alive. However, I suggest you refrain from telling people the part about ripping up money. Instead, so they don't think you're crazy, simply have them read this chapter for themseleves. After reading about this method, they will either be turned on or not. If they're not interested, suggest thc idea to someone else. Almost all of us have things we know we should do, but don't. The I.C.A.N. method really *does* work as well as I say—but only if you use it. Don't let this opportunity to create the life you really want slip away. Either on your own, or (preferably) with anyone you know, begin using this process. In a short period of time, you'll be able to look back on your decision to use this method as a major turning point in your life.

Exactly how do you use an "accountability partner" to stay on track with this process?

When you have found someone else who would like to do this process, decide on a weekly time to meet. Your meeting can be in person or over the phone. During your conversation, ask them if they had any broken agreements. If they did, request that they rip up the appropriate amount of money. Congratulate them for keeping their word. Then they should proceed to ask how you did on *your* contract. Finally, tell your partner the items on your *new* contract, and decide on a specific time to meet or call the following week. That's it. It need not take more than a couple minutes.

Once you're using the I.C.A.N. process, I'd love to hear how it improves your life. Write to me at the address under my biography at the end of this book. If you include a stamped, self-addressed envelope, I'll send you an article on creative, "advanced" ways people have used the I.C.A.N. method to create a magical, prosperous and fulfilling life.

Epilogue

lthough I'm a therapist by profession, I often tell my patients, "A question a day keeps the counselor away." I have always felt it's best for people to learn how to heal and help themselves, rather than depend on someone else to "cure" them. If you ask the questions in this book on a consistent basis, I'm confident you'll notice profound and wonderful results in your life. If you use the I.C.A.N. method outlined in chapter 14 to immediately take action on your answers, you'll notice powerful changes happening at a greatly accelerated rate. Of course, if you're presented with problems of a very serious nature, don't be shy about finding appropriate professional assistance.

Now that you've gone through the book, you might consider writing down several of your favorite questions on a separate piece of paper. This will make it easier for you to ask yourself these questions more regularly. Over the years, I have usually had a list of five or six questions that I ask myself at least once a week to help me stay on track in the various areas of my life. Frequently, I'll ask my friends these same questions as a simple way to help them become happier and more successful. The questions I currently use in this regard are the following:

1) *What could I do that would bring me an even greater sense of fulfillment?*

2) *In the future, what problem might arise in a primary relationship or with my job that I could easily prevent by taking appropriate action now?*

3) *What would I do with a year left to live? Am I doing many of those things in my current life?*

4) *What's going right in my life? What could I feel grateful for?*

5) *What area of life isn't going so well right now? Whom do I know or what resource could I use to get some help with this situation?*

6) *What could I do this week to express love and kindness for the world?*

We live in a speeded-up world in which it's rather easy to get thrown from our deepest dreams and desires. As we venture into the 21st century, the pace of our lives and the changes around us are going to become even more extreme. Fortunately, the questions in this book can do more than help us handle certain troubling situations in our lives. They can also help us develop *faith* in our ability to handle *whatever* life dishes our way. Once we have that faith, we become like an eye of a hurricane, quiet and serene inside despite the raging storm that surrounds us. I hope you'll use these questions to develop a deeper faith in yourself, and a deeper faith in the still, small "voice" within (which some call God). I hope these questions lead you to an even greater appreciation of the miracle and gift of life.

About the Author

Jonathan Robinson is a professional speaker, psychotherapist and seminar leader. For over 20 years, he has specialized in providing people with the most practical and powerful tools available for personal development. Jonathan's work has been featured in *USA Today* and *Newsweek,* and over 200 million people have seen him on shows such as *Oprah, CNN* and *Voice of America.* Mr. Robinson's first book, *Bridges to Heaven: How Well-Known Seekers Deepen Their Connection with God,* included interviews with Mother Teresa, Marianne Williamson, Wayne Dyer, Kenny Loggins, Ram Dass and over 30 other notable spiritual seekers. Jonathan's second book, *The Little Book of Big Questions,* became a bestseller, and provides people with a practical and fun way to explore their spiritual nature.

In seminars and keynote speeches, Robinson is known for using humor and magic illusions to help his audiences remember his practical techniques and empowering message. His talks and workshops include the following:

1) *The Power to Live Your Dream: The Art of Balanced Goal Achievement*

2) *Money Magic: How to Make More While Doing Work You Love*

3) *Experiencing the Sacred in Daily Life*

4) *Communication Magic: How to Solve Problems Without Bruising Egos*

If you would like to receive a free catalog of Robinson's audio- and videotape programs, or wish to discuss a possible workshop or speaking date, please contact him at:

Love Alive Productions
278 Via El Encantador
Santa Barbara, CA 93111
Fax (805) 967-4128